*

By JANE ELIZABETH

Illustrations by Kendrick Drews

Copyright © 2016 Jane Elizabeth

All rights reserved.

ISBN-13: 978-1523344048

DEDICATION

This book is dedicated to all the kids and former kids who love the zoo and think poop is funny, especially Morgan, Hamilton, Aaron and Bryan, who inspired me to think deep thoughts about poop.

Special thanks to family and friends who supported me in many ways during the production of this book, especially Missy, Kelly, Colleen, Eileen, Amy, Rachel, Olivia, and John; to Anita for her brilliance; and to the staff of the Pittsburgh Zoo for a "behind"-the-scenes tour of zoo poop.

This book also is dedicated to the memory of my dad and my brother, both of whom had a fondness for "bathroom jokes" and would have read this book out loud at the dinner table and laughed until milk came out of their noses.

xoxo,

Jane

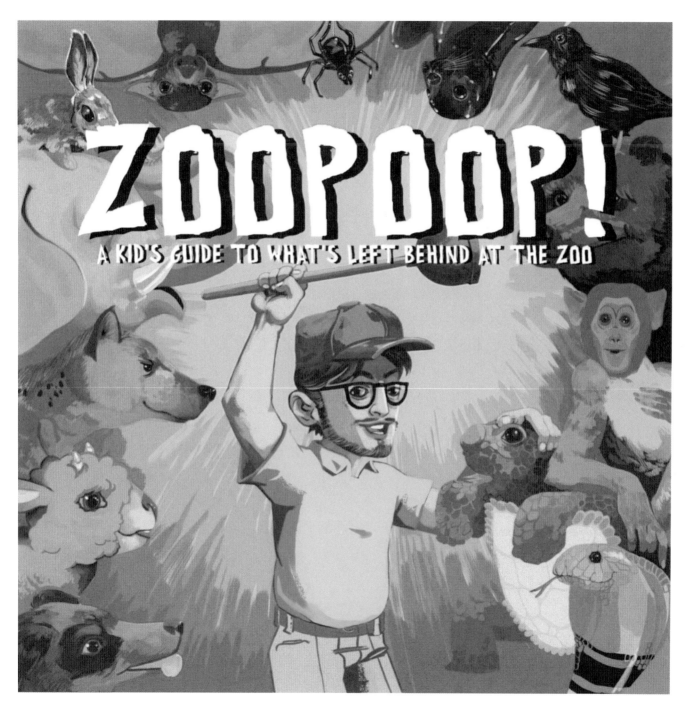

The zoo is a lot of fun, but sometimes it's really SMELLY!

You know why, right?

Yep, it's POOP!

i'm Pops the Plumber, and I'm going to show you some things you can learn from POOP at the ZOO.

Hold your nose, and let's go!

Did you know that POOP
from zoo animals
can be recycled,
just like your cereal boxes and
milk cartons

?

The POOP is swept
off the floor
and put into a special machine
that turns it into fertilizer.

Fertilizer is smelly, too! But it helps grass and flowers and trees grow big and healthy.

Just think, you could even have POOP from the ZOO AT YOUR SCHOOL

Hey, guess who makes some of the BIGGEST POOP at the ZOO

?

Elephants!

They POOP
about once an hour because they can eat
up to 600 pounds of food a day.

By bedtime, they
can make about

300 pounds of POOP!

"What a waste!"
you might say.

But wait! When elephants, gazelles, gorillas
and many other animals eat plants,
seeds drop onto the ground
when they POOP.

The seeds turn into
more plants.

And that means more food for everyone!

You might have guessed this:
An elephant has
one BIG stomach!

The big stomach keeps the
elephants safe
if they eat rocks
or pieces of wood
or the zookeeper's glove.

Yep, that's right:
Elephants will eat almost
ANYTHING!
It just comes out in their
POOP!

Oh, did you know elephants'
teeth come out
in their POOP, too?

Take a look if you dare!

The elephant's big stomach is lazy,
and POOP comes out in a big, messy blob
about the size of a football.

But GAZELLE POOP
is only the size of a prune,
because some zoo animals — like a gazelle or
a camel — have stomachs with many parts
that work hard to turn food into
dry, hard,

small

POOP.

And the CHINCHILLA has some of the
tiniest POOP
you'll ever see.

it's about the size of your pencil tip!

Does CAMEL POOP have two humps?

No, silly! But here's something interesting about camel POOP:

If a camel's POOP comes out stuck together, it could mean it's time for a visit to the doctor!

Zoo animals have check-ups, just like you.

The zoo animals
might have to take
pink medicine for a stomach ache,
just like kids sometimes do.

But an elephant will need about
a dozen bottles!

The zoo doctor
also checks for bad things
in the zoo animals'
POOP,
like worms
or tiny eggs
or blood.

You flush your POOP
down the toilet, right?
But some zoo animals find their own
POOP very useful!

Packrats build their homes
with POOP
and other stuff they find on the
ground.

Then they glue it
all together with
— you guessed it —

PEE!

Monkeys like to play
with their POOP
and even eat their POOP when they get
bored. (But don't worry, it won't hurt them).

Orangutans like to make artwork with
their POOP.
They might make a pattern with their
POOP in the dirt
or even draw on the wall with POOP!

That's our tour of
POOP at the ZOO!

Next time you visit the zoo,
see what you can learn
from the animals' POOP.

And tell them
Pops the Plumber
sent you!

DRAW SOME ZOO POOP HERE!

Color these zoo animals and share your drawing with us!

Ask a grownup to post your drawing on our ZooPoop
Facebook page at
facebook.com/zoopoop

Or send a photo of your drawing to zoopoopbook@gmail.com
and we'll put it on our ZooPoop Facebook page!

And don't forget to tell us all about the zoo animal you drew!

ABOUT THE AUTHOR

Jane Elizabeth is a longtime journalist who has worked at newspapers including The Washington Post, Pittsburgh Post-Gazette, the Virginian-Pilot, and the Richmond Times-Dispatch. She and her husband have four children and six grandchildren, and live in a house on the Chesapeake Bay where you can find poop from deer, foxes and coyotes.

*

Made in the USA
Middletown, DE
06 August 2020